Yard Birds

VERSES ABOUT BIRDS
OBSERVED IN MY YARD

BY
Rachel Bard

ILLUSTRATED BY
Rik Dalvit

Literary Network Press
23817 97th Avenue Southwest
Vashon, Washington 98070
USA

TABLE OF CONTENTS

ALSO BY RACHEL BARD

Navarra, the Durable Kingdom, a history

Newswriting Guide, A Handbook for
Student Reporters

Editing Guide, A Handbook for Writers
and Editors

Best Places of the Olympic Peninsula

Country Inns of the Pacific Northwest

Historical Novels:
  Queen Without a Country
  Isabella: Queen Without a Conscience
  A Reed in the Wind: Joanna Plantagenet,
    Queen of Sicily

FOREWORD

This is not a birdbook. Audubon would have wondered at it and probably scorned it. To the authors of all the commendable contemporary guides, it provides no competition. It's not a field guide to the birds in my yard. The verses and illustrations are for fun, not edification.

These are only a few of the many birds that may be seen here. If there's sufficient popular demand by the three or four readers I hope for, there may be a Volume 2.

Furthermore, you will find a few maritime birds. There's no pond, river or bay in my yard. The largest body of water is the birdbath. But since I live on an island surrounded by Puget Sound, it's a short walk to the shore, which accounts for the cormorant, heron, kingfisher and loon.

Finally, a few birds that I've observed in other countries have flown into these pages when I wasn't looking. I thought they deserved to join the jollity.

So much for disclaimers. Yard Birds, here we come.

STARLING AND ROBIN

A Starling perched on the birdbath rim.
A Robin settled across from him.
His glare meant, "I was first, you know."
Her stare said, "Stupid starling, go!"
They glared and stared for a minute or two.
But he at last said, "Pooh to you,"
And nonchalantly flew away.
She hopped right in, and thought, "I'd say
That starling's manners are the worst.
He ought to know, it's Ladies First."

ROBIN

The Robin cocks her head just so
To learn if there's a worm below.
How clever she to hear the sound
Of that slight wriggle underground.

PINE SISKIN

Pine Siskin is a hearty eater,
Pecking at the birdseed feeder.
All his cousins come and cluster
Till it's like a feather duster.
Belatedly a youngster comes
And finds they've left him only crumbs.
The others jeer and fly away.
"Just be on time, another day."

GREAT DUSKY SWIFT

This I observed at Iguazú:
A flock of Swifts shot from the blue
And headed for the waterfall.
They flew right through it, roar and all,
To find their nest sites, sheltered by
The water curtain. Not so dry,
But safe from any predator.
So that's what waterfalls are for.

Pacific Wren

The modest, shy Pacific Wren
Permits a sighting now and then,
But soon flies off into the wood,
Preferring her own neighborhood.

ANNA'S HUMMINGBIRD

Hummingbirds go darting by,
Bits of rainbow on the fly.

Song Sparrow

Song Sparrows wear a special spot
Smack in the center of the breast.
Thus they announce that they are not
To be confused with all the rest.

GREAT BLUE HERON

Heron stands out in the water,
Luring hapless fish to slaughter.

BELTED KINGFISHER

Kingfisher, perched above the bay,
Swoops on those that got away.

HOUSE CROW

One day in Paris we walked out
To see what birds might be about.
We met a crow beside the Seine.
"Caw, caw!" she cried, then cawed again..
A crust of croissant caught her eye.
A handy puddle was nearby.
She seized the morsel, washed it well,
 Ate half of it, then hopped pell-mell
Across the sidewalk; took a peek
(The soggy remnant in her beak),
Into a clump of grass. Just right!
She hid it there quite out of sight,
And saved it for another day—
Her private corvine IRA.

STARLING

Starlings occupied my lawn
For seven minutes, then were gone.

Steller's Jay

Steller's Jay's a fashion plate.
From regal tail to crested pate.
He gleams in iridescent blue.
I wish his voice were bluesy too,
But when he has something to say,
It comes out as a wheezy bray.

AMERICAN GOLDFINCH

Goldfinch is back. Hooray! It's spring.
I've missed that bird like anything.
He's perched atop the cedar tree,
A fleck of gold for all to see.
Where have you been, fair-feathered friend?
In Mexico? Belize? South Bend?
Not my business? You're so right.
And here's your missus. Future's bright.

CERTIFIED ORGANIC

Red-breasted Nuthatch

Nuthatch prefers a solo lunch,
Far from the rowdy feeder bunch.
He joined them once but fled in panic,
Afraid the seeds were not organic.
Now he forages happily
For bio bugs in the locust tree.

OREGON JUNCO

Juncos keep me company
When, seasonally, others flee.
They flit from hawthorn tree to cedar,
They vie for best spots on the feeder.
You'll seldom see a Junco still.
They gossip, squabble, tweet and trill.
Although their moods go up and down,
I've never seen a Junco frown.
What, never?
Well, hardly ever.

BALD EAGLE

The Eagle, tireless, see him go
Across the great dome of the sky,
Oblivious of those below
As well as other things that fly.

VIOLET-GREEN SWALLOW

When Swallows swoop and glide and soar,
It isn't just for fun.
They've got to find another bug
To feed the little one.

White-crowned Sparrow

White-crowned Sparrow, atop his tree,
Shouts "Whee! Whee! Look at me!"
In case you miss his joyous tweets,
He repeats, repeats, repeats, repeats.

HOUSE SPARROW

English Sparrow was their name,
And they were pleased to be
English birds. But just the same,
They flew across the sea.
House Sparrows now, they're everywhere,
From Utah to Utrecht.
If they were just a bit more rare,
They might get more respect.

Brandt's Cormorant

"Oh cormorant, are you aware
How foolish you look standing there
With wings outstretched as if to say,
'Come, congregation, let us pray'?"

"If I could speak," the bird replied,
"I would explain what you deride.
You see those ducks out in the bay?
They swim and dive the livelong day.

"But when I've caught my fish, then I
Must stand here till my feathers dry.
We cormorants don't have the luck
Of waterproofness, like the duck."

THREE WOODPECKERS

IVORY-BILLED WOODPECKER

Ivory-billed, alas is gone,
Though many claim it lingers on
In some secluded swamp or wood.
And all birders think it should.

PILEATED WOODPECKER
DOWNY WOODPECKER

The Pileated's next in size.
This very day, before my eyes,
One hopped aboard my locust tree
And pecked away most noisily.
Smartly clad in black and white,
Red-crested, it's a gorgeous sight,
Puts tiny Downy in the shade.
No matter. Downy has it made.
He's very small, which means that he
Can squeeze himself quite easily
Into the cage and nibble suet,
While Pileated can't get to it.

Red-winged Blackbird

Six Red-winged Blackbirds landed in the locust.
I'd never seen them in my yard before.
They swarmed the feeder, each one fully focused
On getting its fair share, or maybe more.
The feeder started whirling and gyrating,
As, when it's overloaded, it will do.
The Blackbirds didn't care for that rotating
While they were dining. And so off they flew.
And oh, alas, alack,
They never have come back.

Spotted Towhee

Towhee dear, were you upset
When Goldfinch made State Bird?
You'll get some recognition yet.
Because, bird, have you heard?
Although you may not be far-famed,
You've earned some of your due.
Tahoma Audubon has named
Its newsletter for you!

COMMON LOON

The Loons, they tell us, mate for life.
Some primal inner force
Keeps them as husband and as wife,
With no thought of divorce.

Black-capped Chickadee

One day I watched a Chickadee
Who hopped about the locust tree.
She tasted insects she found there
To see if they were proper fare.
Carefully evaluating,
As though she gave each branch a rating.
She flew off to another tree,
Still diligently on patrol.
I speculated. Could it be
She's charged with Quality Control?

THE RAVEN

Quoth the Raven,
No more, please!

AFTERWORD

Perhaps it occurs to some readers that birds should be taken more seriously. Many poets think so. And so may the birds. I've selected a few of my favorite bird poems by highly respected poets. This will give the reader some relief from all the frivolity.

SIX SERIOUS BIRD POEMS

Migrant   Albin Fabian 2015

MIGRANT

by Mary Kollar

There is no battle there
At the end of our frozen bay,
but a surrender to wonder.
Where summer-long the purple martins sang
now a great snowy owl, tundra-born
clutches a cedar snag.

Her plumage is like a dandelion blown.
Her song a foreign clicking of tongue.

She has flown half the earth
and day to night may fly farther
than we who think we've settled here,
reading wisdom in her eternal stare
over tidal land she claims
simply because she arrived.

HOPE IS THE THING WITH FEATHERS

By Emily Dickinson

"Hope" is the thing with feathers -
That perches on the soul -
And sings the tune without the words -
And never stops at all -

And sweetest in the Gale is heard –
And sore must be the storm –
That could abash the little Bird
That kept so many warm -

I've heard it in the chillest land –
And on the strangest Sea –

Yet, never in Extremity,
It asked a crumb – of Me.

AUGURIES OF INNOCENCE

by William Blake (excerpts)

To see a World in a Grain of Sand
And a Heaven in a Wild Flower,
Hold Infinity in the palm of your hand
And Eternity in an hour.

A Robin Red breast in a Cage
Puts all Heaven in a Rage.
A dove house fill'd with doves and Pigeons
Shudders Hell thro' all its regions.

A Skylark wounded in the wing,
A Cherubim does cease to sing.
The Game Cock clip'd and armed for fight
Does the rising Sun affright.

The Owl that calls upon the Night
Speaks the Unbeliever's fright.
He who shall hurt the little Wren
Shall never be belov'd by Men.

AUBADE

By William Shakespeare

Hark! Hark! The lark at heaven's gate sings,
And Phoebus 'gins arise,
His steeds to water at those springs
On chaliced flowers that lies;
And winking Mary-buds begin
To ope their golden eyes;
With everything that pretty bin,
My lady sweet, arise!
Arise, arise!

TITWILLOW

By W. S. Gilbert (from "The Mikado")

On a tree by a river a little tomtit
Sang "Willow, titwillow, titwillow!"
And I said to him, "Dicky-bird, why do you sit
Singing,"Willow, titwillow, titwillow!"
"Is it weakness of intellect, birdie?" I cried,
"Or a rather tough worm in your little inside?"
With a shake of his poor little head he replied,
"Oh, Willow, titwillow, titwillow!"

Corvus Seattlensis No. 2, by Rebecca Roush ©

DUST OF SNOW

By Robert Frost

The way a crow
Shook down on me
The dust of snow
From a hemlock tree
Has given my heart
A change of mood
And saved some part
Of a day I had rued.

ACKNOWLEDGEMENTS

p. 52, "Migrant," silkscreen print, permission of Allan Kollar. Copyrighted.

p. 53 "Migrant" permission of Mary Kollar. Copyrighted.

pp. 54-57 William Shakespeare and William Blake agreed to their poems' use but asked, "What's a copyright?" W.S. Gilbert and Emily Dickenson gladly gave permission and knew what a copyright is, but were sure theirs had expired.

p. 58 Rebecca Roush says Corvus Seattlensis is made of beads, sequins, felt, crow's feet, pewter charm in beak. She says no crows were harmed in any way. She found the deceased crow at the side of the road. She believes this crow is flying toward the hemlock to shake some snow on Robert Frost.

p. 59 Robert Frost said of course he knows what a copyright is, and this poem entered the public domain before 1923. Even a crow knows that.

Thanks to all the above. And to Rik Dalvit for bravely undertaking the illustrations and for his uncanny ability to find in the verses what's funny and to depict it with humor and clarity.

And to Chris Craven, who understands and can deal with those abstruse details like how many dpi and sizing an illustration. And to Paula Gill, who designed the whole book: front and back covers, the text, and the arrangement of the illustrations. She got the book in perfect shape for publication. And to Randy Robinson, bird authority par excellence, for setting me straight on the correct current names of the birds.

About Us

After eight works of nonfiction and three historical novels, Rachel Bard decided it was time for a little amusement. She began writing short verses about the birds she saw from her home on Vashon Island. The birds inhabited or visited two cedars, a hawthorn, a yew, a locust, a dogwood, a birdbath, and two birdhouses. But the busiest gathering places were the birdseed feeder and the suet cage. By the time she had two dozen or so verses, she thought that they might make a book. And they did.

Editorial cartoonist and bird lover Rik Dalvit flew at the chance to illustrate Rachel Bard's whimsical bird verses, finding them a refreshing change from his usual subjects. His drawings were inspired by her witty observations.